ISBN 978-0-243-46658-0
PIBN 10800500

Forgotten Books is a registered trademark of FB &c Ltd.
Copyright © 2018 FB &c Ltd.
FB &c Ltd, Dalton House, 60 Windsor Avenue, London, SW19 2RR.
Company number 08720141. Registered in England and Wales.

For support please visit www.forgottenbooks.com

1 MONTH OF
FREE
READING

at

www.ForgottenBooks.com

By purchasing this book you are eligible for one month membership to ForgottenBooks.com, giving you unlimited access to our entire collection of over 1,000,000 titles via our web site and mobile apps.

To claim your free month visit:
www.forgottenbooks.com/free800500

English
Français
Deutsche
Italiano
Español
Português

www.forgottenbooks.com

Mythology Photography **Fiction**
Fishing Christianity **Art** Cooking
Essays Buddhism Freemasonry
Medicine **Biology** Music **Ancient
Egypt** Evolution Carpentry Physics
Dance Geology **Mathematics** Fitness
Shakespeare **Folklore** Yoga Marketing
Confidence Immortality Biographies
Poetry **Psychology** Witchcraft
Electronics Chemistry History **Law**
Accounting **Philosophy** Anthropology
Alchemy Drama Quantum Mechanics
Atheism Sexual Health **Ancient History**
Entrepreneurship Languages Sport
Paleontology Needlework Islam
Metaphysics Investment Archaeology
Parenting Statistics Criminology
Motivational

AFTER STRANGE GODS

A PRIMER
OF MODERN HERESY

THE PAGE-BARBOUR LECTURES
AT THE UNIVERSITY OF VIRGINIA
1933

BY

T. S. ELIOT

καὶ ταῦτ' ἰὼν
εἴσω λογίζου· κἂν λάβῃς ἐψευσμένον,
φάσκειν ἔμ' ἤδη μαντικῇ μηδὲν φρονεῖν.
—*Œdipus Rex :* l. 460-462.

LONDON
FABER AND FABER LIMITED
24 RUSSELL SQUARE

FIRST PUBLISHED IN FEBRUARY MCMXXXIV
BY FABER AND FABER LIMITED
24 RUSSELL SQUARE LONDON W.C.I
SECOND IMPRESSION NOVEMBER MCMXXXIV
PRINTED IN GREAT BRITAIN BY
R. MACLEHOSE AND COMPANY LIMITED
THE UNIVERSITY PRESS GLASGOW
ALL RIGHTS RESERVED

To

ALFRED and ADA SHEFFIELD

Das Chaos in der 'Literatur', die mit vagen Grenzen zwar, aber immer noch deutlicher ein Gebiet für sich ist; sie, die in gesunden Zeiten ein relativ reiner, gefälliger Spiegel aller herschenden Dinge und Undinge ist, in kranken, chaotischen ein selber trüber all der trüben Dinge und Ideen, die es gibt, ist zur cloaca maxima geworden. Jegliche Unordnung im Humanen, im Menschen selber—ich sprach von dem dreifachen Gesichtspunkt, unter dem sie betrachtet werden kann, dem Primat der Lust, dem Primat der Sentimentalität, dem Primat der technischen Intelligenz—an Stelle der einzig wahren hierarchischen Ord-) nung, des Primates des Geistes und des Spiritualen—jegliche Unordnung findet ihr relativ klares oder meist selber noch neuerlich verzerrtes Bild in der Literatur dieser Tage.

—THEODOR HAECKER: *Was ist der Mensch?* p. 65.

PREFACE

*L*e *monde moderne avilit.* It also provincialises, and it can also corrupt.

The three lectures which follow were not undertaken as exercises in literary criticism. If the reader insists upon considering them as such, I should like to guard against misunderstanding as far as possible. The lectures are not designed to set forth, even in the most summary form, my opinions of the work of contemporary writers: they are concerned with certain ideas in illustration of which I have drawn upon the work of some of the few modern writers whose work I know. I am not primarily concerned either with their absolute importance or their importance relatively to each other; and other writers, who in any literary survey of our time ought to be included, are unmentioned or barely mentioned, because they do not provide such felicitous illustration of my thesis, or because they are rare exceptions to it, or because I am unacquainted with their work. I am sure that those whom I have discussed are among the best; and for my purpose the second-rate were useless. The extent to which I have criticised the authors whose names find place, is accordingly some measure of my x respect for them. I dare say that a detached critic could find an equally rich vein of error in my own writings. If such error is there, I am probably the last person to be able to

detect it; but its presence and discovery would not condemn what I say here, any more than its absence would
confirm it.

There is no doubt some curiosity to know what any
writer thinks of his contemporaries: a curiosity which has
less to do with literary criticism than with literary gossip.
I hope that a reader who takes up this essay in that expec-
tation will be disappointed. I am uncertain of my ability to
criticise my contemporaries as artists; I ascended the platform of these lectures only in the role of moralist.

I have not attempted to disguise, but rather have been
pleased to remind the reader, that these are lectures; that
they were composed for vocal communication to a particular audience. What the Foundation requires is that the
lectures shall be published, not that a book shall subse-
quently be written on the same subject; and a lecture composed for the platform cannot be transformed into something else. I should be glad if the reader could keep this in
mind when he finds that some ideas are put forward
without a full account of their history or of their activities,
and that others are set down in an absolute way without
qualifications. I am aware that my assertion of the obsol-
escence of Blasphemy might thus be subject to stricture:
but if I had developed the refinements and limitations which
present themselves to the mind of the Christian enquirer,
I should have needed at least the space of one whole
lecture; and what I was concerned to do was merely to
explain that the charge of blasphemy was *not* one of those
that I wished to prefer against modern literature. It may be
said that no blasphemy can be purely verbal; and it may

12

also be said that there is a profounder meaning of the term 'blasphemy', in which some modern authors (including, possibly, myself) may possibly have been gravely guilty.

In such matters, as perhaps in everything, I must depend upon some good-will on the part of the reader. I do not wish to preach only to the converted, but primarily to those who, never having applied moral principles to literature quite explicitly—perhaps even having conscientiously believed that they ought not to apply them in this way to 'works of art'—are possibly convertible. I am not arguing or reasoning, or engaging in controversy with those whose views are radically opposed to such as mine. In our time, controversy seems to me, on really fundamental matters, to be futile. It can only usefully be practised where there is common understanding. It requires common assumptions; and perhaps the assumptions that are only felt are more important than those that can be formulated. The acrimony which accompanies much debate is a symptom of differences so large that there is nothing to argue about. We experience such profound differences with some of our contemporaries, that the nearest parallel is the difference between the mentality of one epoch and another. In a society like ours, worm-eaten with Liberalism, the only thing possible for a person with strong convictions is to state a point of view and leave it at that.

I wish to express my thanks to Professor Wilbur Nelson and the Page-Barbour Lectureship Committee; to the Acting President and the members of the Faculty of the University of Virginia who helped to make my visit to

Virginia a very pleasant memory; to my hosts, Professor and Mrs. Scott Buchanan; to Professor Buchanan for conversations and suggestions out of which these lectures arose; and to the Revd. M. C. D'Arcy, S.J., and Mr. F. V. Morley for their criticisms. It is a pleasure to me to think that these lectures were delivered at one of the older, smaller and most gracious of American educational institutions, one of those in which some vestiges of a traditional education seem to survive. Perhaps I am mistaken: but if not, I should wish that I might be able to encourage such institutions to maintain their communications with the past, because in so doing they will be maintaining their communications with any future worth communicating with.

T. S. E.

London, January 1934.

I

Some years ago I wrote an essay entitled *Tradition and the Individual Talent.* During the course of the subsequent fifteen years I have discovered, or had brought to my attention, some unsatisfactory phrasing and at least one more than doubtful analogy. But I do not repudiate what I wrote in that essay any more fully than I should expect to do after such a lapse of time. The problem, naturally, does not seem to me so simple as it seemed then, nor could I treat it now as a purely literary one. What I propose to attempt in these three lectures is to outline the matter as I now conceive it.

It seemed to me appropriate to take this occasion, my first visit to Virginia, for my re-formulation. You have here, I imagine, at least some recollection of a 'tradition', such as the influx of foreign populations has almost effaced in some parts of the North, and such as never established itself in the West: though it is hardly to be expected that a tradition here, any more than anywhere else, should be found in healthy and flourishing growth. I have been much interested, since the publication a few years ago of a book called *I'll Take My Stand,* in what is sometimes called the agrarian movement in the South, and I look forward to any further statements by the same group of writers.

May I say that my first, and no doubt superficial im-
pressions of your country—I speak as a New Englander—
have strengthened my feeling of sympathy with those authors: no one, surely, can cross the Potomac for the first
time without being struck by differences so great that their
extinction could only mean the death of both cultures. I
had previously been led to wonder, in travelling from
Boston to New York, at what point Connecticut ceases to
be a New England state and is transformed into a New
York suburb; but to cross into Virginia is as definite an
experience as to cross from England to Wales, almost as
definite as to cross the English Channel. And the differences
here, with no difference of language or race to support
them, have had to survive the immense pressure towards
monotony exerted by the industrial expansion of the latter
part of the nineteenth and the first part of the twentieth
century. The Civil War was certainly the greatest disaster
in the whole of American history; it is just as certainly a
disaster from which the country has never recovered, and
perhaps never will: we are always too ready to assume
that the good effects of wars, if any, abide permanently
while the ill-effects are obliterated by time. Yet I think that
the chances for the re-establishment of a native culture are
perhaps better here than in New England. You are farther
away from New York; you have been less industrialised
and less invaded by foreign races; and you have a more
opulent soil.

My local feelings were stirred very sadly by my first view
of New England, on arriving from Montreal, and journey-
ing all one day through the beautiful desolate country of

Vermont. Those hills had once, I suppose, been covered with primæval forest; the forest was razed to make sheep pastures for the English settlers; now the sheep are gone, and most of the descendants of the settlers; and a new forest appeared blazing with the melancholy glory of October maple and beech and birch scattered among the evergreens; and after this procession of scarlet and gold and purple wilderness you descend to the sordor of the half-dead mill towns of southern New Hampshire and Massachusetts. It is not necessarily those lands which are the most fertile or most favoured in climate that seem to me the happiest, but those in which a long struggle of adaptation between man and his environment has brought out the best qualities of both; in which the landscape has been moulded by numerous generations of one race, and in which the landscape in turn has modified the race to its own character. And those New England mountains seemed to me to give evidence of a human success so meagre and transitory as to be more desperate than the desert.

I know very well that the aim of the 'neo-agrarians' in the South will be qualified as quixotic, as a hopeless stand for a cause which was lost long before they were born. It will be said that the whole current of economic determin-ism is against them, and economic determinism is to-day a god before whom we fall down and worship with all kinds of music. I believe that these matters may ultimately be determined by what people want; that when anything is generally accepted as desirable, economic laws can be upset in order to achieve it; that it does not so much matter at present whether any measures put forward are practical, as

whether the aim is a good aim, and the alternatives inrol-
erable. There are, at the present stage, more serious difficulties in the revival or establishment of a tradition and a way
of life, which require immediate consideration.

Tradition is not solely, or even primarily, the maintenance of certain dogmatic beliefs; these beliefs have come
to take their living form in the course of the formation of a
tradition. What I mean by tradition involves all those
habitual actions, habits and customs, from the most significant religious rite to our conventional way of greeting a
stranger, which represent the blood kinship of 'the same
people living in the same place'. It involves a good deal
which can be called *taboo*: that this word is used in our time
in an exclusively derogatory sense is to me a curiosity
of some significance. We become conscious of these
items, or conscious of their importance, usually only after
they have begun to fall into desuetude, as we are aware of
the leaves of a tree when the autumn wind begins to blow
them off—when they have separately ceased to be vital.
Energy may be wasted at that point in a frantic endeavour
to collect the leaves as they fall and gum them onto the
branches: but the sound tree will put forth new leaves, and
the dry tree should be put to the axe. We are always in
danger, in clinging to an old tradition, or attempting to
re-establish one, of confusing the vital and the unessential,
the real and the sentimental. Our second danger is to associate tradition with the immovable; to think of it as
something hostile to all change; to aim to return to some
previous condition which we imagine as having been
capable of preservation in perpetuity, instead of aiming

18

to stimulate the life which produced that condition in its time.

It is not of advantage to us to indulge a sentimental attitude towards the past. For one thing, in even the very best living tradition there is always a mixture of good and bad, and much that deserves criticism; and for another, tradition is not a matter of feeling alone. Nor can we safely, without very critical examination, dig ourselves in stubbornly to a few dogmatic notions, for what is a healthy belief at one time may, unless it is one of the few fundamental things, be a pernicious prejudice at another. Nor should we cling to traditions as a way of asserting our superiority over less favoured peoples. What we can do is to use our minds, remembering that a tradition without intelligence is not worth having, to discover what is the best life for us not as a political abstraction, but as a particular people in a particular place; what in the past is worth preserving and what should be rejected; and what conditions, within our power to bring about, would foster the society that we desire. Stability is obviously necessary. You are hardly likely to develop tradition except where the bulk of the population is relatively so well off where it is that it has no incentive or pressure to move about. The population should be homogeneous ; where two or more cultures exist in the same place they are likely either to be fiercely self-conscious or both to become adulterate.[1] What is still

[1]Or else you may get a *caste* system, based on original distinctions of race, as in India: which is a very different matter from *classes*, which pre-suppose homogeneity of race and a fundamental equality. But social classes, as distinct from economic classes, hardly exist to-day.

more important is unity of religious background; and reasons of race and religion combine to make any large number of free-thinking Jews undesirable. There must be a proper balance between urban and rural, industrial and agricultural development. And a spirit of excessive tolerance is to be deprecated. We must also remember that—in spite of every means of transport that can be devised—the local community must always be the most permanent, and that the concept of the nation is by no means fixed and invariable.[1] It is, so to speak, only one fluctuating circle of loyalties between the centre of the family and the local community, and the periphery of humanity entire. Its strength and its geographical size depend upon the comprehensiveness of a way of life which can harmonise parts with distinct local characters of their own. When it becomes no more than a centralised machinery it may affect some of its parts to their detriment, or to what they believe to be their detriment; and we get the regional movements which have appeared within recent years. It is only a law of nature, that local patriotism, when it represents a distinct tradition and culture, takes precedence over a more abstract national patriotism. This remark should carry more weight for being uttered by a Yankee.

So far I have only pronounced a few doctrines all of

[1] 'To place the redemptive work of the Christian Faith in social affairs in its proper setting, it is necessary to have clearly in mind at the outset that the consciousness of "the nation" as *the* social unit is a very recent and contingent experience. It belongs to a limited historical period and is bound up with certain specific happenings, theories of society and attitudes to life as a whole.' V. A. Demant, *God, Man and Society*, p. 146.

which have been developed by other writers.[1] I do not intend to trespass upon their fields. I wished simply to indicate the connotation which the term *tradition* has for me, before proceeding to associate it with the concept of *orthodoxy*, which seems to me more fundamental (with its opposite, *heterodoxy*, for which I shall also use the term *heresy*) than the pair *classicism—romanticism* which is frequently used.

As we use the term *tradition* to include a good deal more than 'traditional religious beliefs', so I am here giving the term *orthodoxy* a similar inclusiveness; and though of course I believe that a right tradition for us must be also a Christian tradition, and that orthodoxy in general implies Christian orthodoxy, I do not propose to lead the present series of lectures to a theological conclusion. The relation between tradition and orthodoxy in the past is evident enough; as is also the great difference there may be between an orthodox Christian and a member of the Tory Party. But Conservatism, so far as it has ever existed, so far as it has ever been intelligent, and not merely one of the names for hand-to-mouth party politics, has been associated with the defence of tradition, ideally if not often in fact. On the other hand, there was certainly, a hundred years ago, a relation between the Liberalism which attacked the

---

[1] I should not like to hold any one of them responsible for my opinions, however, or for any that the reader may find irritating. I have in mind Mr. Chesterton and his 'distributism', Mr. Christopher Dawson (*The Making of Europe*), Mr. Demant and Mr. M. B. Reckitt and their colleagues. I have also in mind the views of Mr. Allen Tate and his friends as evinced in *I'll Take My Stand*, and those of several Scottish nationalists.

Church and the Liberalism which appeared in politics. According to a contemporary, William Palmer, the former group of Liberals

'were eager to eliminate from the Prayer-book the belief in the Scriptures, the Creeds, the Atonement, the worship of Christ. They called for the admission of Unitarian infidels as fellow-believers. They would eviscerate the Prayer-book, reduce the Articles to a deistic formulary, abolish all subscriptions or adhesions to formularies, and reduce religion to a state of anarchy and dissolution. These notions were widely spread. They were advocated in numberless publications, and greedily received by a democratic, thoughtless public. . . . Christianity, as it had existed for eighteen centuries, was unrepresented in this turmoil.'[1]

It is well to remember that this sort of Liberalism was flourishing a century ago; it is also well to remember that it is flourishing still. Not many months ago I read an article by an eminent liberal divine from which I have preserved the following sentence:

'We now have at hand an apparatus which, though not yet able to discover reality, is fully competent to identify and to eliminate the disproportionate mass of error which has found lodgment in our creeds and codes. The factual untruth and the fallacious inference are being steadily eliminated from the hereditary body of religious faith and moral practice.'

And, in order not to limit my instances to theology, I will quote from another contemporary Liberal practitioner, a literary critic this time:

'Aided by psycho-analysis, which gave them new wea-

[1] Quoted in *Northern Catholicism*, p. 9.

22

pons, many of the poets and dramatists of our day have dug into the most perverse of human complexes, exposing them with the scalpel of a surgeon rather than that of a philosopher.'

At this point I may do well to anticipate a possible misunderstanding. In applying the standard of orthodoxy to contemporary literature my emphasis will be upon its collective rather than its static meaning. A superficial apprehension of the term might suggest the assumption that everything worth saying has been said, and that the possible forms of expression have all been discovered and developed; the assumption that novelty of form and of substance was always to be deprecated. What is objectionable, from the point of view which I have adopted, is not novelty or originality in themselves, but their glorification for their own sake. The artist's concern with originality, certainly, may be considered as largely negative: he wishes only to avoid saying what has already been said as well as it can be. But I am not here occupied with the standards, ideals and rules which the artist or writer should set before himself, but with the way in which his work should be taken by the reader; not with the aberrations of writers, but with those of readers and critics. To assert that a work is 'original' should be very modest praise: it should be no more than to say that the work is not patently negligible. Contemporary literature may conveniently be divided as follows. There is first that which attempts to do what has already been done perfectly, and it is to this superfluous kind of writing that the word 'traditional' is commonly applied: mis-applied, for the word itself implies a movement. Tradition cannot mean standing still. Of course, no writer ever admits to himself that he has *no* originality; but the fact that a writer can be satisfied to use the exact idiom of a predecessor is very suspicious; you cannot write satire in the line of Pope or the stanza of Byron. The second kind of contemporary writing aims at an exaggerated novelty, a novelty usually of a trifling kind, which conceals from the uncritical reader a fundamental commonplaceness. If you examine the works of any great innovator in chronological order, you may expect to find that the author has been driven on, step by step, in his innovations, by an inner necessity, and that the novelty of form has rather been forced upon him by his material than deliberately sought. It is well also to remember that what any one writer can contribute in the way of 'originality' is very small indeed, and has often a pitifully small relation to the mass of his writings.

As for the small number of writers, in this or any other period, who are worth taking seriously, I am very far from asserting that any of these is wholly 'orthodox' or even that it would be relevant to rank them according to degrees of orthodoxy. It is not fair, for one thing, to judge the individual by what can be actual only in society as a whole; and most of us are heretical in one way or another. Nor is the responsibility solely with the individual. Furthermore, the essential of any important heresy is not simply that it is wrong: it is that it is partly right. It is characteristic of the more interesting heretics, in the context in which I use the term, that they have an exceptionally acute perception, or profound insight, of some part of the truth; an insight more important often than the inferences of those who are aware of more but less acutely aware of anything. So far as we are able to redress the balance, effect the compensation, ourselves, we may find such authors of the greatest value. If we value them as they value themselves we shall go astray. And in the present state of affairs, with the low degree of education to be expected of public and of reviewers, we are more likely to go wrong than right ; we must remember too, that an heresy is apt to have a seductive simplicity, to make a direct and persuasive appeal to intellect and emotions, and to be altogether more plausible than the truth.

It will already have been observed that my contrast of heresy and orthodoxy has some analogy to the more usual one of romanticism and classicism; and I wish to emphasise this analogy myself, as a safeguard against carrying it too far. I would wish in any case to make the point that romanticism and classicism are not matters with which creative writers can afford to bother over much, or with which they do, as a rule, in practice greatly concern themselves. It is true that from time to time writers have labelled themselves 'romanticists' or 'classicists', just as they have from time to time banded themselves together under other names. These names which groups of writers and artists give themselves are the delight of professors and historians of literature, but should not be taken very seriously; their chief value is temporary and political—that, simply, of helping to make the authors known to a contemporary public; and I doubt whether any poet has ever done himself anything but harm by attempting to write as a 'romantic' or as a 'classicist'.

No sensible author, in the midst of something that he is trying to write, can stop to consider whether it is going to be romantic or the opposite. At the moment when one writes, one is what one is, and the damage of a lifetime, and of having been born into an unsettled society, cannot be repaired at the moment of composition.

The danger of using terms like 'romantic' and 'classic'—this does not however give us permission to avoid them altogether—does not spring so much from the confusion caused by those who use these terms about their own work, as from inevitable shifts of meaning in context. We do not mean quite the same thing when we speak of a writer as romantic, as we do when we speak of a literary period as romantic. Furthermore, we may have in mind, on any particular occasion, certain virtues or vices more or less justly associated with one term or the other, and it is doubtful whether there is any total sum of virtues or of vices which may be arrogated to either class. The opportunities for systematic misunderstanding, and for futile controversy, are accordingly almost ideal; and discussion of the subject is generally conducted by excitement of passion and prejudice, rather than by reason. Finally—and this is the most important point—the differences represented by these two terms are not such as can be confined to a purely literary context. In using them, you are ultimately bringing in all human values, and according to your own scheme of valuation. A thorough-going classicist is likely to be a thorough-going individualist, like the late Irving Babbitt; so that one should be on guard, in using such terms, against being thorough-going.

When we press such a term to an exactness which it will not bear, confusions are bound to occur. Such, for instance, is the association sometimes made between classicism and Catholicism. It is possible for a man to adhere to both; but he should not be under the delusion that the connexion is necessarily objective: it may spring from some unity within himself, but that unity, as it is in him, may not be valid for the rest of the world. And you cannot treat on the same 'footing the maintenance of religious and literary principles. I have said that you cannot restrict the terms 'romantic' and 'classical', as professors of literature conveniently do, to the literary context; but on the other hand you cannot wholly free them from that context either. There is surely something wrong when a critic divides all works of art neatly into one group and the other and then plumps for the romantic or the classical as a whole. Whichever you like in theory, it is suspicious if you prefer works altogether of one class in practice: probably you have either made the terms merely names for what you admire and for what you dislike, or you have forced and falsified your tastes.[1] Here again is the error of being too thorough-going.

I may as well admit at this point that in this discussion of terms I have my own log to roll. Some years ago, in the preface to a small volume of essays, I made a sort of summary declaration of faith in matters religious, political and literary. The facility with which this statement has been quoted has helped to reveal to me that as it stands the

[1] For instance: two of my own favourite authors are Sir Thomas Malory and Racine.

statement is injudicious. It may suggest that the three sub-
jects are of equal importance to me, which is not so; it may
suggest that I accept all three beliefs on the same grounds,
which is not so; and it may suggest that I believe that they
all hang together or fall together, which would be the
most serious misunderstanding of all. That there are con-
nexions for me I of course admit, but these illuminate my
own mind rather than the external world; and I now see
the danger of suggesting to outsiders that the Faith is a
political principle or a literary fashion, and the sum of all a
dramatic posture.

From another aspect also I have a personal interest in the
clearing up of the use of the terms with which I have been
concerned. My friend Dr. Paul Elmer More is not the first
critic to call attention to an apparent incoherence between
my verse and my critical prose—though he is the first whose
perplexity on this account has caused me any distress. It
would appear that while I maintain the most correct opinions in my criticism, I do nothing but violate them in my
verse; and thus appear in a double, if not double-faced role.
I feel no shame in this matter. I am not of course interested
by those critics who praise my criticism in order to discredit my verse, or those who praise my verse in order to
discredit my opinions in religious or social affairs; I am only
interested in answering those critics who, like Dr. More,
have paid me the compliment—deserved or not does not
here matter—of expressing some approval of both. I
should say that in one's prose reflexions one may be legiti-
mately occupied with ideals, whereas in the writing of
verse one can only deal with actuality. Why, I would ask,

is most religious verse so bad; and why does so little religious verse reach the highest levels of poetry? Largely, I think, because of a pious insincerity. The capacity for writing poetry is rare; the capacity for religious emotion of the first intensity is rare; and it is to be expected that the existence of both capacities in the same individual should be rarer still. People who write devotional verse are usually writing as they want to feel, rather than as they do feel. Likewise, in an age like the present, it could only be poetry of the very greatest rank that could be genuinely what Dr. More would be obliged to call 'classical'; poets of lower ability—that is all but such as half a dozen perhaps in the world's history—could only be 'classical' by being pseudo-classical; by being unfaithful and dishonest to their experience. It should hardly be necessary to add that the 'classical' is just as unpredictable as the romantic, and that most of us would not recognise a classical writer if he appeared, so queer and horrifying he would seem even to those who clamour for him.

I hold—in summing up—that a *tradition* is rather a way of feeling and acting which characterises a group throughout generations; and that it must largely be, or that many of the elements in it must be, unconscious; whereas the maintenance of *orthodoxy* is a matter which calls for the exercise of all our conscious intelligence. The two will therefore considerably complement each other. Not only is it possible to conceive of a tradition being definitely bad; a good tradition might, in changing circumstances, become out of date. Tradition has not the means to criticise itself; it may perpetuate much that is trivial or of transient significance

as well as what is vital and permanent. And while tradition, being a matter of good habits, is necessarily real
only in a social group, orthodoxy exists whether realised in
anyone's thought or not. Orthodoxy also, of course represents a consensus between the living and the dead: but a
whole generation might conceivably pass without any
orthodox thought; or, as by Athanasius, orthodoxy may
be upheld by one man against the world. Tradition may be
conceived as a by-product of right living, not to be aimed
at directly. It is of the blood, so to speak, rather than of the
brain: it is the means by which the vitality of the past en-
riches the life of the present. In the co-operation of both is
the reconciliation of thought and feeling. The concepts of
romantic and classic are both more limited in scope and less
definite in meaning. Accordingly they do not carry with
them the implication of absolute value which those who
have defended one against the other would give them: it is
only in particular contexts that they can be contrasted in
this way, and there are always values more important than
any that either of these terms can adequately represent. I
propose in my second lecture to illustrate these general reflexions by some application to modern English literature.

II

I hope that it is quite clear, both for the sake of what I have said already and for the sake of what I have still to say, that the sense in which I am using the terms *tradition* and *orthodoxy* is to be kept distinctly in mind as not identical with the use of the same terms in theology. The difference is widest with the term *tradition*, for I have wished to use the word to cover much in our lives that is accounted for by habit, breeding and environment. I should not on the other hand like to have it supposed that my meanings were arbitrarily chosen. That they bear a relation to the more exact meanings I have no wish to conceal: if they did not, my discussion of these matters would lose all significance. But the two terms have been so frequently and so subtly expounded by more philosophical writers, that I would guard against being thought to employ, in a loose and in-expert manner, terms which have already been fully and sharply defined. With the terms in their theological use I shall presume no acquaintance; and I appeal only to your common-sense: or, if that word sounds too common, to your wisdom and experience of life. That an acceptance of the validity of the two terms as I use them should lead one to dogmatic theology, I naturally believe; but I am not here concerned with pursuing investigation in that path. My enquiries take the opposite direction: let us consider

the denial or neglect of tradition in my mundane sense, and
see what *that* leads to.

The general effect in literature of the lack of any strong
tradition is twofold: extreme individualism in views, and
no accepted rules or opinions as to the limitations of the
literary job. I have spoken elsewhere[1] of poetry as a sub-
stitute for religion, and of kinds of criticism which assumed
that the function of poetry was to replace religion. The
two results are naturally concomitant. When one man's
'view of life' is as good as another's, all the more enterprising spirits will naturally evolve their own; and where
there is no custom to determine what the task of literature
is, every writer will determine for himself, and the more
enterprising will range as far afield as possible. But at this
point I should develop one distinction between the usual
sense of 'orthodoxy' and that in which it is here used. I do
not take orthodoxy to mean that there is a narrow path
laid down for every writer to follow. Even in the stricter
discipline of the Church, we hardly expect every theolo-
gian to succeed in being orthodox in every particular, for
it is not a sum of theologians, but the Church itself, in
which orthodoxy resides. In my sense of the term, perfect
orthodoxy in the individual artist is not always necessary,
or even desirable. In many instances it is possible that an
indulgence of eccentricities is the condition of the man's
saying anything at all. It is impossible to separate the
'poetry' in *Paradise Lost* from the peculiar doctrines that it
enshrines; it means very little to assert that if Milton had
held more normal doctrines he would have written a

[1] In *The Use of Poetry*.

better poem; as a work of literature, we take it as we find
it: but we can certainly enjoy the poetry and yet be fully
aware of the intellectual and moral aberrations of the
author. It is true that the existence of a right tradition,
simply by its influence upon the environment in which the
poet develops, will tend to restrict eccentricity to manage-
able limits: but it is not even by the lack of this restraining
influence that the absence of tradition is most deplorable.
What is disastrous is that the writer should deliberately
give rein to his 'individuality', that he should even culti-
vate his differences from others; and that his readers should
cherish the author of genius, not in spite of his deviations
from the inherited wisdom of the race, but because of
them.

What happens is not, to be sure, always just what the
author intends. It is fatally easy, under the conditions of the
modern world, for a writer of genius to conceive of himself as a Messiah. Other writers, indeed, may have had profound insights before him; but we readily believe that
everything is relative to its period of society, and that these
insights have now lost their validity; a new generation is
a new world, so there is always a chance, if not of delivering a wholly new gospel, of delivering one as good as new.
Or the messiahship may take the form of revealing for the
first time the gospel of some dead sage, which no one has
understood before; which owing to the backward and con-
fused state of men's minds has lain unknown to this very
moment; or it may even go back to the lost Atlantis and
the ineffable wisdom of primitive peoples. A writer who is
fired with such a conviction is likely to have some devoted

disciples; but for posterity he is liable to become, what he will be for the majority of his contemporaries, merely one among many entertainers. And the pity is that the man *may* have had something to say of the greatest importance: but to announce, as your own discovery, some truth long known to mankind, is to secure immediate attention at the price of ultimate neglect.

The general effect upon readers—most of them quite uneducated—is quite different from what the serious messiah intends. In the first place, no modern messiah can last for more than a generation; it is tacitly assumed that the leaders of the previous generation are as useless as the soldiers who died in the first year of a hundred years' war (and alas, they mostly are); those who enjoy the normal span of life may be sure of surviving their popularity. Secondly, as the public is not very well qualified for discriminating between nostrums, it comes to enjoy sampling all, and taking none seriously. And finally, in a world that has as nearly lost all understanding of the meaning of *education* as it well can, many people act upon the assumption that the mere accumulation of 'experiences', including literary and intellectual experiences, as well as amorous and picaresque ones, is—like the accumulation of money—valuable in itself. So that a serious writer may sweat blood over his work, and be appreciated as the exponent of still one more 'point of view'.

It is too much to expect any literary artist at the present time to be a model of orthodoxy. That, as I have said, is something to demand only in a spirit of indulgent criticism at any time: it is not to be demanded now. It is a very different thing to be a classical author in a classical age, and to maintain classical ideals in a romantic age. Furthermore, I ask the same compassion for myself that I would have you extend to others. What we can try to do is to develop a more critical spirit, or rather to apply to authors critical standards which are almost in desuetude. Of the contemporary authors whom I shall mention, I cannot recall having seen any criticism in which these standards have been employed.

Perhaps it will make the foregoing considerations appear more real, and exonerate me from the charge of dealing only in abstractions, offering only a kind of unredeemable paper currency, if at this point I give testimony in the form of three contemporary short stories, all of very great merit. It was almost by accident that I happened to read all of these stories in rapid succession during the course of some recent work at Harvard. One is B*liss* by Katherine Mansfield; the second is _The Shadow in the Rose Garden_ by D. H. Lawrence, and the third *The Dead* by James Joyce.[1] They are all, I believe, fairly youthful work; and all turn on the same theme of disillusion. In Miss Mansfield's story a wife is disillusioned about her relations with her husband; in the others a husband is disillusioned about his relations with his wife. Miss Mansfield's story—it is one of her best known—is brief, poignant and in the best sense, slight; Mr. Joyce's is of considerable length. What is interesting in the three together is the differences of moral implication. In B*liss*, I should say, the moral implication is negligible:

[1]From volumes entitled *Bliss, The Prussian Officer,* and *Dubliners* respectively.

the centre of interest is the wife's feeling, first of ecstatic happiness, and then at the moment of revelation. We are given neither comment nor suggestion of any moral issue of good and evil, and within the setting this is quite right. The story is limited to this sudden change of feeling, and the moral and social ramifications are outside of the terms of reference. As the material is limited in this way—and indeed our satisfaction recognises the skill with which the author has handled perfectly the *minimum* material—it is what I believe would be called feminine. In the story of Lawrence there is a great deal more than that; he is concerned with the feelings of both husband and wife; and as the tempo is much slower (no story of any considerable structure could move as rapidly as Miss Mansfield's does) there is time for thought as well as feeling, and for calculated action. An accident, trifling in itself, but important in the twist which Lawrence gives to it, leads or forces the wife to reveal to her commonplace lower middle-class husband (no writer is more conscious of class-distinctions than Lawrence) the facts of her intrigue with an army officer several years before their marriage. The disclosure is made with something nearly approaching conscious cruelty. There is cruelty, too, in the circumstances in which she had met her former lover:

'"And I saw him to-day," she said. "He is not dead, he's mad." Her husband looked at her, startled. "Mad!" he said involuntarily. "A lunatic," she said.'

Of this alarming strain of cruelty in some modern literature I shall have something more to say later. What I wish chiefly to notice at this point, is what strikes me in all of the

relations of Lawrence's men and women: the absence of
any moral or social sense. It is not that the author, in that
Olympian elevation and superior indifference attributed to
great artists, and which I can only imperfectly understand,
has detached himself from any moral attitude towards his
characters; it is that the characters themselves, who are supposed to be recognisably human beings, betray no respect
for, or even awareness of, moral obligations, and seem to
be unfurnished with even the most commonplace kind of
conscience. In Mr. Joyce's story, which is very much
longer and which incidentally employs a much more elaborate and interesting method, the wife is saddened by
memories associated with a song sung at an evening party
which has just been described in minute detail. In response
to solicitous questions by her husband, she reveals the fact
that the song had been sung by a boy she knew in Galway
when she was a girl, and that between them was an intense
romantic and spiritualised love. She had had to go away;
the boy had risen from a sick bed to come to say goodbye
to her; and he had in consequence died. That is all there
was to it; but the husband realises that what this boy had
given her was something finer than anything he had to
give. And as the wife falls asleep at last:

'Generous tears filled Gabriel's eyes. He had never felt like
that himself towards any woman, but he knew that such a
feeling must be love. The tears gathered more thickly in
his eyes and in the partial darkness he imagined he saw the
form of a young man standing under a dripping tree.
Other forms were near. His soul had approached that
region where dwell the vast hosts of the dead.'

It is impossible to produce the full value of evidence such
as this without reading the stories entire; but something of
what I have in mind should now be apparent. We are not
concerned with the authors' *beliefs*, but with orthodoxy of
sensibility and with the sense of tradition, our degree of
approaching 'that region where dwell the vast hosts of the
dead'. And Lawrence is for my purposes, an almost perfect
example of the heretic. And the most ethically orthodox of
the more eminent writers of my time is Mr. Joyce. I con-
fess that I do not know what to make of a generation
which ignores these considerations.

I trust that I shall not be taken as speaking in a spirit of
bigotry when I assert that the chief clue to the understanding of most contemporary Anglo-Saxon literature is to be
found in the decay of Protestantism. I am not concerned
with Protestantism itself: and to discuss that we should
have to go back to the seventeenth century. I mean that
amongst writers the rejection of Christianity—Protestant
Christianity—is the rule rather than the exception; and
that individual writers can be understood and classified
according to the type of Protestantism which surrounded
their infancy, and the precise state of decay which it
had reached. I should include those authors who were
reared in an 'advanced' or agnostic atmosphere, because
even agnosticism—*Protestant* agnosticism—has decayed
in the last two generations. It is this background, I believe, that makes much of our writing seem provincial
and crude in the major intellectual centres of Europe—
everywhere except northern Germany and perhaps Scan-
dinavia; it is this which contributes the prevailing flavour of

immaturity. One might expect the unlovelier forms of this decline to be more deeply marked upon American authors than upon English, but there is no reason to generalise: nothing could be much drearier (so far as one can judge from his own account) than the vague hymn-singing pietism which seems to have consoled the miseries of Lawrence's mother, and which does not seem to have provided her with any firm principles by which to scrutinise the conduct of her sons. But lest I be supposed to be concerned primarily with the decay of morals (and especially sexual morals) I will mention the name of one for whose memory I have the highest respect and admiration: that of the late Irving Babbitt.

It is significant to observe that Babbitt was saturated with French culture; in his thought and in his intercourse he was thoroughly cosmopolitan. He believed in tradition; for many years he stood almost alone in maintaining against the strong tendency of the time a right theory of education; and such effects of decadence as are manifest in Lawrence's work he held in abomination. And yet to my mind the very width of his culture, his intelligent eclecticism, are themselves symptoms of a narrowness of tradition, in their extreme reaction against that narrowness. His attitude towards Christianity seems to me that of a man who had had no *emotional* acquaintance with any but some debased and uncultured form: I judge entirely on his public pronouncements and not at all on any information about his upbringing. It would be exaggeration to say that he wore his cosmopolitanism like a man who had lost his *complet bourgeois* and had to go about in fancy dress. But he seemed to be trying to compensate for the lack of living tradition by a herculean, but purely intellectual and individual effort. His addiction to the philosophy of Confucius is evidence: the popularity of Confucius among our contemporaries is significant. Just as I do not see how anyone can expect really to understand Kant and Hegel without knowing the German language and without such an understanding of the German mind as can only be acquired in the society of living Germans, so *a fortiori* I do not see how anyone can understand Confucius without some knowledge of Chinese and a long frequentation of the best Chinese society. I have the highest respect for the Chinese mind and for Chinese civilisation; and I am willing to believe that Chinese civilisation at its highest has graces and excellences which may make Europe seem crude. But I do not believe that I, for one, could ever come to understand it well enough to make Confucius a mainstay.

I am led to this conclusion partly by an analogous experience. Two years spent in the study of Sanskrit under Charles Lanman, and a year in the mazes of Patanjali's metaphysics under the guidance of James Woods, left me in a state of enlightened mystification. A good half of the effort of understanding what the Indian philosophers were after—and their subtleties make most of the great European philosophers look like schoolboys—lay in trying to erase from my mind all the categories and kinds of distinction common to European philosophy from the time of the Greeks. My previous and concomitant study of European philosophy was hardly better than an obstacle. And I came to the conclusion—seeing also that the 'influence' of Brah-

min and Buddhist thought upon Europe, as in Schopen-
hauer, Hartmann, and Deussen, had largely been through
romantic misunderstanding—that my only hope of really
penetrating to the heart of that mystery would lie in for-
getting how to think and feel as an American or a European: which, for practical as well as sentimental reasons, I
did not wish to do. And I should imagine that the same
choice would hold good for Chinese thought: though I believe that the Chinese mind is very much nearer to the
Anglo-Saxon than is the Indian. China is—or was until the
missionaries initiated her into Western thought, and so
blazed a path for John Dewey—a country of tradition;
Confucius was not born into a vacuum; and a network of
rites and customs, even if regarded by philosophers in a
spirit of benignant scepticism, make a world of difference.
But Confucius has become the philosopher of the rebellious
Protestant. And I cannot but feel that in some respects
Irving Babbitt, with the noblest intentions, has merely
made matters worse instead of better.

The name of Irving Babbitt instantly suggests that of
Ezra Pound (his peer in cosmopolitanism) and that of I. A.
Richards: it would seem that Confucius is the spiritual
adviser of the highly educated and fastidious, in contrast to
the dark gods of Mexico. Mr. Pound presents the closest
counterpart to Irving Babbitt. Extremely quick-witted and
very learned, he is attracted to the Middle Ages, apparently,
by everything except that which gives them their significance. His powerful and narrow post-Protestant prejudice
peeps out from the most unexpected places: one can hardly
read the erudite notes and commentary to his edition of

Guido Cavalcanti without suspecting that he finds Guido much more sympathetic than Dante, and on grounds which have little to do with their respective merits as poets: namely, that Guido was very likely a heretic, if not a sceptic —as evidenced partly by his possibly having held some pneumatic philosophy and theory of corpuscular action which I am unable to understand. Mr. Pound, like Babbitt, is an individualist, and still more a libertarian.

Mr. Pound's theological twist appears both in his poetry and his prose; but as there are other vigorous prose writers, and as Mr. Pound is probably the most important living poet in our language, a reference to his poetry will carry more weight. At this point I shall venture to generalise, and suggest that with the disappearance of the idea of Original Sin, with the disappearance of the idea of intense moral struggle, the human beings presented to us both in poetry and in prose fiction to-day, and more patently among the serious writers than in the underworld of letters, tend to become less and less real. It is in fact in moments of moral and spiritual struggle depending upon spiritual sanctions, rather than in those 'bewildering minutes' in which we are all very much alike, that men and women come nearest to being real. If you do away with this struggle, and maintain that by tolerance, benevolence, inoffensiveness and a re-distribution or increase of purchasing power, combined with a devotion, on the part of an élite, to Art, the world will be as good as anyone could require, then you must expect human beings to become more and more vaporous. This is exactly what we find of the society which Mr. Pound puts in Hell, in his *Draft of XXX Cantos*. It consists (I may have

overlooked one or two species) of politicians, profiteers,
financiers, newspaper proprietors and their hired men,
agents provocateurs, Calvin, St. Clement of Alexandria, the
English, vice-crusaders, liars, the stupid, pedants, preachers,
those who do not believe in Social Credit, bishops, lady
golfers, Fabians, conservatives and imperialists; and all
'those who have set money-lust before the pleasures of the
senses'. It is, in its way, an admirable Hell, 'without dignity, without tragedy'. At first sight the variety of types—
for these are types, and not individuals—may be a little
confusing; but I think it becomes a little more intelligible
if we see at work three principles, (1) the aesthetic, (2) the
humanitarian, (3) the Protestant. And I find one considerable objection to a Hell of this sort: that a Hell altogether
without dignity implies a Heaven without dignity also. If
you do not distinguish between individual responsibility
and circumstances in Hell, between essential Evil and social
accidents, then the Heaven (if any) implied will be equally
trivial and accidental. Mr. Pound's Hell, for all its horrors,
is a perfectly comfortable one for the modern mind to con-
template, and disturbing to no one's complacency: it is a
Hell for the *other people*, the people we read about in the
newspapers, not for oneself and one's friends.[1]

An equally interesting example of the modern mind is
that of the other important poet of our time, Mr. William
Butler Yeats. Few poets have told us more about themselves—more, I mean, of what is relevant and of what we
are entitled to know—than Mr. Yeats in his 'Autobio-
graphies', a document of great and permanent interest. Mr.

[1]Consult *Time and Western Man* by Wyndham Lewis.

Yeats had still greater difficulties to contend with, I should say, than Mr. Pound. He was born of Irish Protestant stock, and was brought up in London; Ireland was for his childhood rather a holiday country, to which his sentiment attached itself; his father adhered to mid-century Rationalism, but otherwise the household atmosphere was Pre-Raphaelite. In *The Trembling of the Veil* he says significantly:

'I was unlike others of my generation in one thing only. I am very religious, and deprived by Huxley and Tyndall, whom I detested, of the simple-minded religion of my childhood, I had made a new religion, almost an infallible church of poetic tradition, of a fardel of stories, and of personages, and of emotions, inseparable from their first expression, passed on from generation to generation by poets and painters with some help from philosophers and theologians.' Thus, in Yeats at the age of sixteen (or at least, as in retrospect he seems to himself to have been at sixteen) is operative the doctrine of Arnold, that Poetry can replace Religion; and also the tendency to fabricate an *individual* religion. The rationalistic background, the Pre-Raphaelite imagery, the interest in the occult, the equally early interest in Irish nationalism, the association with minor poets in London and Paris, make a curious mixture. Mr. Yeats was in search of a tradition, a little too consciously perhaps—like all of us. He sought for it in the conception of Ireland as an autonomous political and social unity, purged from the Anglo-Saxon pollution. He wished also to find access to the religious sources of poetry, as, a little later, did another restless seeker for myths, D. H. Lawrence. The result, for a long period, is a somewhat artificially induced poeticality. Just

44

as much of Swinburne's verse has the effect of repeated doses of gin and water, so much of Mr. Yeats's verse is stimulated by folklore, occultism, mythology and symbolism, crystal-gazing and hermetic writings.

> 'Who will go drive with Fergus now,
> And pierce the deep wood's woven shade,
> And dance upon the level shore?
> Young man, lift up your russet brow,
> And lift your tender eyelids, maid,
> And brood on hopes and fears no more.'

This is to me very beautiful but highly artificial. There is a deliberate evocation of trance, as he virtually confesses in his essay on *The Symbolism of Poetry*:

'The purpose of rhythm, it has always seemed to me, is to prolong the moment of contemplation, the moment when we are both asleep and awake, which is the one moment of creation, by hushing us with an alluring monotony, while it holds us waking by its variety, to keep us in that state of perhaps real trance, in which the mind liberated from the pressure of the will is unfolded in symbols.'
There is a good deal of truth in this theory, but not quite enough, and its practice exposes Mr. Yeats to the just criticism of Mr. I. A. Richards, as follows:

'After a drawn battle with the drama, Mr. Yeats made a violent repudiation, not merely of current civilisation but of life itself, in favour of a supernatural world. But the world of the "eternal moods", of supernal essences and immortal beings is not, like the Irish peasant stories and the Irish landscape, part of his natural and familiar experience.

45

Now he turns to a world of symbolic phantasmagoria about which he is desperately uncertain. He is uncertain because he has adopted as a technique of inspiration the use of trance, of dissociated phases of consciousness, and the revelations given in these dissociated states are insufficiently connected with normal experience.'

It is, I think, only carrying Mr. Richards's complaint a little further to add that Mr. Yeats's 'supernatural world' was the wrong supernatural world. It was not a world of spiritual significance, not a world of real Good and Evil, of holiness or sin, but a highly sophisticated lower mythology summoned, like a physician, to supply the fading pulse of poetry with some transient stimulant so that the dying patient may utter his last words. In its extreme self-consciousness it approaches the mythology of D. H. Lawrence on its more decadent side. We admire Mr. Yeats for having outgrown it; for having packed away his bibelots and resigned himself to live in an apartment furnished in the barest simplicity. A few faded beauties remain: Babylon, Nineveh, Helen of Troy, and such souvenirs of youth: but the austerity of Mr. Yeats's later verse on the whole, should compel the admiration of the least sympathetic. Though the tone is often of regret, sometimes of resignation:

> 'Things said or done long years ago,
> Or things I did not do or say
> But thought that I might say or do,
> Weigh me down, and not a day
> But something is recalled,
> My conscience or my vanity appalled.'

and though Mr. Yeats is still perhaps a little too much the weather-worn Triton among the streams, he has arrived at greatness against the greatest odds; if he has not arrived at a central and universal philosophy he has at least discarded, for the most part, the trifling and eccentric, the provincial in time and place.

At this point, having called attention to the difficulties experienced by Mr. Pound and Mr. Yeats through no fault of their own, you may be expecting that I shall produce Gerard Hopkins, with an air of triumph, as the orthodox and traditional poet. I wish indeed that I could; but I cannot altogether share the enthusiasm which many critics feel for this poet, or put him on a level with those whom I have just mentioned. In the first place, the fact that he was a Jesuit priest, and the author of some very beautiful devotional verse, is only partially relevant. To be converted, in any case, while it is sufficient for entertaining the hope of individual salvation, is not going to do for a man, as a writer, what his ancestry and his country for some generations have failed to do. Hopkins is a fine poet, to be sure; but he is not nearly so much a poet of our time as the accidents of his publication and the inventions of his metric have led us to suppose. His innovations certainly were good, but like the mind of their author, they operate only within a narrow range, and are easily imitated though not adaptable for many purposes; furthermore, they sometimes strike me as lacking inevitability—that is to say, they sometimes come near to being purely *verbal*, in that a whole poem will give us *more* of the same thing, an accumulation, rather than a real development of thought or feeling.

I may be wrong about Hopkins's metric and vocabulary. But I am sure that in the matter of devotional poetry a good deal more is at issue than just the purity and strength of the author's devotional passion. To be a 'devotional poet' is a limitation: a saint limits himself by writing poetry, and a poet who confines himself to even this subject matter is limiting himself too. Hopkins is not a religious poet in the more important sense in which I have elsewhere maintained Baudelaire to be a religious poet; or in the sense in which I find Villon to be a religious poet; or in the sense in which I consider Mr. Joyce's work to be penetrated with Christian feeling. I do not wish to depreciate him, but to affirm limitations and distinctions. He should be compared, not with our contemporaries whose situation is different from his, but with the minor poet nearest contemporary to him, and most like him: George Meredith. The comparison is altogether to Hopkins's advantage. They are both English nature poets, they have similar technical tricks, and Hopkins is much the more agile. And where Meredith, beyond a few acute and pertly expressed observations of human nature, has only a rather cheap and shallow 'philosophy of life' to offer, Hopkins has the dignity of the Church behind him, and is consequently in closer contact with reality. But from the struggle of our time to concentrate, not to dissipate; to renew our association with traditional wisdom; to re-establish a vital connexion between the individual and the race; the struggle, in a word, against Liberalism: from all this Hopkins is a little apart, and in this Hopkins has very little aid to offer us.

What I have wished to illustrate, by reference to the authors whom I have mentioned in this lecture, has been the crippling effect upon men of letters, of not having been born and brought up in the environment of a living and central tradition. In the following lecture I shall be concerned rather with the positive effects of heresy, and with much more alarming consequences: those resulting from exposure to the diabolic influence.

III

I think that there is an interesting subject of investigation, for the student of traditions, in the history of Blasphemy, and the anomalous position of that term in the modern world. It is a curious survival in a society which has for the most part ceased to be capable of exercising that activity or of recognising it. I am persuaded that pretty generally, when that term is used at all, it is used in a sense which is only the shadow of the original. For modern blasphemy is merely a department of bad form: just as, in countries which still possess a Crown, people are usually (and quite rightly) shocked by any public impertinence concerning any member of their Royal Family, they are still shocked by any public impertinence towards a Deity for whom they feel privately no respect at all; and both feelings are supported by the conservatism of those who have anything to lose by social changes. Yet people nowadays are inclined to tolerate and respect any violation which is presented to them as inspired by 'serious' purposes; whereas the only disinfectant which makes either blasphemy or obscenity sufferable is the sense of humour: the indecent that is funny may be the legitimate source of innocent merriment, while the absence of humour reveals it as purely disgusting.

I do not wish to be understood as undertaking a defence

of blasphemy in the abstract. I am only pointing out that it is a very different thing in the modern world from what it would be in an 'age of faith'; just as a magistrate's conception of blasphemy will probably be very different from that of a good Catholic, and his objections to it will be for very different reasons. The whole question of censorship is now of course reduced to ludicrous inconsistency, and is likely to remain so as long as the morals of the State are not those of the Church. But my point is that blasphemy is not a matter of good form but of right belief; no one can possibly blaspheme in any sense except that in which a parrot may be said to curse, unless he profoundly believes in that which he profanes; and when anyone who is not a believer is shocked by blasphemy he is shocked merely by a breach of good form; and it is a nice question whether, being in a state of intellectual error, he is or is not committing a sin in being shocked for the wrong reasons. It is certainly my opinion that first-rate blasphemy is one of the rarest things in literature, for it requires both literary genius and profound faith, joined in a mind in a peculiar and unusual state of spiritual sickness. I repeat that I am not defending blasphemy; I am reproaching a world in which blasphemy is impossible.

My next point is a more delicate one to handle. One can conceive of blasphemy as doing moral harm to feeble or perverse souls; at the same time one must recognise that the modern environment is so unfavourable to faith that it produces fewer and fewer individuals capable of being injured by blasphemy. One would expect, therefore, that (whatever it may have been at other times) blasphemy would be less employed by the Forces of Evil than at any other time in the last two thousand years.' Where blasphemy might once have been a sign of spiritual corruption, it might now be taken rather as a symptom that the soul is still alive, or even that it is recovering animation: for the perception of Good and Evil—whatever choice we may make—is the first requisite of spiritual life.) We should do well, therefore, to look elsewhere than to the blasphemer, in the traditional sense, for the most fruitful operations of the Evil Spirit to-day.

I regret, for my present purposes, that I have not a more intimate, accurate and extensive knowledge of the English novelists of the last hundred years, and that therefore I feel a little insecure of my generalisations. But it seems to me that the eminent novelists who are more nearly contemporary to us, have been more concerned than their predecessors—consciously or not—to impose upon their readers their own *personal view of life*, and that this is merely part of the whole movement of several centuries towards the aggrandisement and exploitation of *personality*. I do not suggest that 'personality' is an illicit intruder; I imagine that the admirers of Jane Austen are all fascinated by something that may be called her personality. But personality, with Jane Austen, with Dickens and with Thackeray, was more nearly in its proper place. The standards by which they criticised their world, if not very lofty ones, were at least not of their own making. In Dickens's novels, for instance, the religion is still of the good old torpid eighteenth century kind, dressed up with a profusion of holly and turkey, and supplemented by strong humanitarian

zeal. These novelists were still observers: however superficial—in contrast, for instance, to Flaubert—we find their
observations to be. They are orthodox enough according
to the light of their day: the first suspicion of heresy creeps in
with a writer who, at her best, had much profounder moral
insight and passion than these, but who unfortunately combined it with the dreary rationalism of the epoch of which
she is one of the most colossal monuments: George Eliot.
George Eliot seems to me of the same tribe as all the serious
and eccentric moralists we have had since: we must respect
her for being a serious moralist, but deplore her individual-
istic morals. What I have been leading up to is the following assertion: that when morals cease to be a matter of
tradition and orthodoxy—that is, of the habits of the community formulated, corrected, and elevated by the con-
tinuous thought and direction of the Church—and when
each man is to elaborate his own, then *personality* becomes a
thing of alarming importance.

The work of the late Thomas Hardy represents an interesting example of a powerful personality uncurbed by any
institutional attachment or by submission to any objective
beliefs; unhampered by any ideas, or even by what sometimes acts as a partial restraint upon inferior writers, the
desire to please a large public. He seems to me to have
written as nearly for the sake of 'self-expression' as a man
well can; and the self which he had to express does not strike
me as a particularly wholesome or edifying matter of communication. He was indifferent even to the prescripts of
good writing: he wrote sometimes overpoweringly well,
but always very carelessly; at times his style touches sub-

limity without ever having passed through the stage of
being good. In consequence of his self-absorption, he makes
a great deal of landscape; for landscape is a passive creature
which lends itself to an author's mood. Landscape is fitted
too for the purposes of an author who is interested not at
all in men's minds, but only in their emotions; and perhaps
only in men as vehicles for emotions. It is only, indeed,
in their emotional paroxysms that most of Hardy's characters come alive. This extreme emotionalism seems to me
a symptom of decadence; it is a cardinal point of faith in a
romantic age, to believe that there is something admirable
in violent emotion for its own sake, whatever the emotion
or whatever its object. But it is by no means self-evident that
human beings are most real when most violently excited;
violent physical passions do not in themselves differentiate
men from each other, but rather tend to reduce them to the
same state; and the passion has significance only in relation
to the character and behaviour of the man at other moments of his life and in other contexts. Furthermore, strong
passion is only interesting or significant in strong men;
those who abandon themselves without resistance to ex-
citements which tend to deprive them of reason, become
merely instruments of feeling and lose their humanity; and
unless there is moral resistance and conflict there is no
meaning. But as the majority is capable neither of strong
emotion nor of strong resistance, it always inclines to
admire passion for its own sake, unless instructed to the
contrary; and, if somewhat deficient in vitality, people
imagine passion to be the surest evidence of vitality. This in
itself may go towards accounting for Hardy's popularity.

What again and again introduces a note of falsity into Hardy's novels is that he will leave nothing to nature, but will always be giving one last turn of the screw himself, and of his motives for so doing I have the gravest suspicion. In *The Mayor of Casterbridge*—which has always seemed to me his finest novel as a whole—he comes the nearest to producing an air of inevitability, and of making the crises seem the consequences of the character of Henchard; the arrangement by which the hero, leaning over a bridge, finds himself staring at his effigy in the stream below is a masterly *tour de force*. This scene is however as much by arrangement as less successful ones in which the motive intrudes itself more visibly; as for instance the scene in *Far From The Madding Crowd* in which Bathsheba unscrews Fanny Robin's coffin—which seems to me deliberately faked. And by this I mean that the author seems to be deliberately relieving some emotion of his own at the expense of the reader. It is a refined form of torture on the part of the writer, and a refined form of self-torture on the part of the reader. And this brings me to the point of this lecture, for the first time.

I have not so far made it apparent what relation the documents considered in this lecture bear to the subject matter of the last. I was there concerned with illustrating the limiting and crippling effect of a separation from tradition and orthodoxy upon certain writers whom I nevertheless hold up for admiration for what they have attempted against great obstacles. Here I am concerned with the intrusion of the *diabolic* into modern literature in consequence of the same lamentable state of affairs; and it was for this

reason that I took the pains at the beginning to point out
that blasphemy is not a matter with which we are concerned. I am afraid that even if you can entertain the notion
of a positive power for evil working through human
agency, you may still have a very inaccurate notion of
what Evil is, and will find it difficult to believe that it
may operate through men of genius of the most excellent
character. I doubt whether what I am saying can convey
very much to anyone for whom the doctrine of Original
Sin is not a very real and tremendous thing. I can only ask
you to read the texts, and then reconsider my remarks.
And one of the most significant of the Hardy texts is a
volume of short stories, indeed of masterly short stories,
which has never received enough examination from that
point of view: I mean *A Group of Noble Dames*. Here, for
one thing, you get essential Hardy without the Wessex
staging; without the scenery dear to the Anglo-Saxon
heart or the period peasants pleasing to the metropolitan
imagination. Not all of these stories, of course, illustrate
my point equally well; the best for my purpose, to which I
refer you, rather than take up your time by summarising
the plot, is *Barbara of the House of Grebe*. This is not realism;
it is as Hardy catalogues it, 'romance and fantasy' with
which Hardy can do exactly what he wants to do. I do not
object to horror: *Œdipus Rex* is a most horrible plot from
which the last drop of horror is extracted by the dramatist;
and among Hardy's contemporaries, Conrad's *Heart of
Darkness* and James's *Turn of the Screw* are tales of horror.
But there is horror in the real world; and in these works
of Sophocles, Conrad and James we are in a world of

Good and Evil. In *Barbara of the House of Grebe* we are introduced into a world of pure Evil. The tale would seem to have been written solely to provide a satisfaction for some morbid emotion.

I find this same strain in the work of a man whose morbidity I have already had occasion to mention, and whom I regard as a very much greater genius, if not a greater artist, than Hardy: D. H. Lawrence. Lawrence has three aspects, and it is very difficult to do justice to all. I do not expect to be able to do so. The first is the ridiculous: his lack of sense of humour, a certain snobbery, a lack not so much of information as of the critical faculties which education should give, and an incapacity for what we ordinarily call thinking. Of this side of Lawrence, the brilliant exposure by Mr. Wyndham Lewis in *Paleface* is by far the most conclusive criticism that has been made. Secondly, there is the extraordinarily keen sensibility and capacity for profound intuition—intuition from which he commonly drew the wrong conclusions. Third, there is a distinct sexual morbidity. Unfortunately, it is necessary to keep all of these aspects in mind in order to criticise the writer fairly; and this, in such close perspective, is almost impossible. I shall no doubt appear to give excessive prominence to the third; but that, after all, is what has been least successfully considered.

I have already touched upon the deplorable religious upbringing which gave Lawrence his lust for intellectual independence: like most people who do nor know what orthodoxy is, he hated it. With the more intimate reasons, of heredity and environment, for eccentricity of thought and feeling I am not concerned: too many people have made them their business already. And I have already mentioned the insensibility to ordinary social morality, which is so alien to my mind that I am completely baffled by it as a monstrosity. The point is that Lawrence started life wholly free from any restriction of tradition or institution, that he had no guidance except the Inner Light, the most untrustworthy and deceitful guide that ever offered itself to wandering humanity. It was peculiarly so for Lawrence, who does not appear to have been gifted with the faculty of self-criticism, except in flashes, even to the extent of ordinary wordly shrewdness. Of divine illumination, it may be said that probably every man knows when he has it, but that any man is likely to think that he has it when he has it not; and even when he has had it, the daily man that he is may draw the wrong conclusions from the enlightenment which the momentary man has received: no one, in short, can be the sole judge of whence his inspiration comes. A man like Lawrence, therefore, with his acute sensibility, violent prejudices and passions, and lack of intellectual and social training, is admirably fitted to be an instrument for forces of good or for forces of evil; or as we might expect, partly for one and partly for the other. A trained mind like that of Mr. Joyce is always aware what master it is serving; an untrained mind, and a soul destitute of humility and filled with self-righteousness, is a blind servant and a fatal leader. It would seem that for Lawrence any spiritual force was good, and that evil resided only in the absence of spirituality. Most people, no doubt, need to be aroused to the perception of the simple distinction between the spiritual and

the material; and Lawrence never forgot, and never mis-
took, this distinction. But most people are only very little
alive; and to awaken them to the spiritual is a very great
responsibility: it is only when they are so awakened that
they are capable of real Good, but that at the same time
they become first capable of Evil.) Lawrence lived all his
life, I should imagine, on the spiritual level; no man was
less a sensualist. Against the living death of modern
material civilisation he spoke again and again, and even if
these dead could speak, what he said is unanswerable. As a
criticism of the modern world, *Fantasia of the Unconscious*
is a book to keep at hand and re-read. In contrast to Not-
tingham, London or industrial America, his capering red-
skins of *Mornings in Mexico* seem to represent Life. So they
do; but that is not the last word, only the first.

The man's vision is spiritual, but spiritually sick.
The dæmonic powers found an instrument of far greater
range, delicacy and power in the author of *The Prussian
Officer* than in the author of *A Group of Noble Dames*;
and the tale which I used as an example (*The Shadow
in the Rose Garden*) can be matched by several others.
I have not read all of his late and his posthumous
works, which are numerous. In some respects, he may
have progressed: his early belief in Life may have passed
over, as a really serious belief in Life must, into a belief
in Death.[1] But I cannot see much development in
Lady Chatterley's Lover. Our old acquaintance, the game-
keeper, turns up again: the social obsession which makes

---

[1] I am indebted to an unpublished essay by Mr. E. F. W. Tomlin for
the suggestion that this is so.

his well-born—or almost well-born—ladies offer themselves to—or make use of—plebeians springs from the same
morbidity which makes other of his female characters be-
stow their favours upon savages. The author of that book
seems to me to have been a very sick man indeed.

There is, I believe, a very great deal to be learned from
Lawrence; though those who are most capable of exercising the judgement necessary to extract the lesson, may not
be those who are most in need of it. That we can and ought
to reconcile ourselves to Liberalism, Progress and Modern
Civilisation is a proposition which we need not have
waited for Lawrence to condemn; and it matters a good
deal in what name we condemn it. I fear that Lawrence's work may appeal, not to those who are well and
able to discriminate, but to the sick and debile and con-
fused; and will appeal not to what remains of health in
them, but to their sickness. Nor will many even accept his
doctrine as he would give it, but will be busy after their
own inventions. The number of people in possession of any
criteria for discriminating between good and evil is very
small; the number of the half-alive hungry for any form of
spiritual experience, or what offers itself as spiritual experience, high or low, good or bad, is considerable. My own
generation has not served them very well. Never has the
printing-press been so busy, and never have such varieties of
buncombe and false doctrine come from it. *Woe unto the
foolish prophets, that follow their own spirit, and have seen
nothing! O Israel, thy prophets have been like foxes in the waste
places. . . . And the word of the* LORD *came unto me, saying,
Son of man, these men have taken their idols into their hearts,*

*and put the stumbling-block of their iniquity before their face:
should I be inquired of at all by them?*

I wish to add a few words of retrospect and summary,
partly as a reminder of how little, in the space of three
hours, one can undertake to say about such a serious subject as this. In an age of unsettled beliefs and enfeebled
tradition the man of letters, the poet, and the novelist, are
in a situation dangerous for themselves and for their
readers. I tried to safeguard myself, in my first lecture, from
being taken to be merely a sentimental admirer of some
real or imaginary past, and from being taken as a faker of
traditions. Tradition by itself is not enough; it must be
perpetually criticised and brought up to date under the
supervision of what I call orthodoxy; and for the lack of
this supervision it is now the sentimental tenuity that we
find it. Most 'defenders of tradition' are mere conservatives, unable to distinguish between the permanent and the
temporary, the essential and the accidental. But I left this
theory as a bare outline, to serve as a background for my
illustration of the dangers of authorship to-day. Where
there is no external test of the validity of a writer's work,
we fail to distinguish between the truth of his view of life
and the personality which makes it plausible; so that in our
reading, we may be simply yielding ourselves to one seductive personality after another. The first requisite usually
held up by the promoters of personality is that a man
should 'be himself'; and this 'sincerity' is considered more
important than that the self in question should, socially and
spiritually, be a good or a bad one. This view of person-

ality is merely an assumption on the part of the modern world, and is no more tenable than several other views which have been held at various times and in several places. The personality thus expressed, the personality which fascinates us in the work of philosophy or art, tends naturally to be the *unregenerate* personality, partly self-deceived and partly irresponsible, and because of its freedom, terribly *limited* by prejudice and self-conceit, capable of much good or great mischief according to the natural goodness or impurity of the man: and we are all, naturally, impure. All that I have been able to do here is to suggest that there are standards of criticism, not ordinarily in use, which we may apply to whatever is offered to us as works of philosophy or of art, which might help to render them safer and more profitable for us.

APPENDIX

I have after some deliberation called this essay a primer of modern heresy: hinting that it is offered primarily to those who may be interested in pursuing the subject by themselves. I had thought of supplementing it by a graduated Exercise Book, beginning with very simple examples of heresy, and leading up to those which are very difficult to solve; and leaving the student to find the answers for himself. My chief reason for abandoning this project is perhaps the overwhelming abundance of elementary exercises, compared with the paucity of those which can tax the abilities of the really quick and proficient student. I therefore content myself with four examples. No. I is very elementary: countless specimens of the same kind might be found. No. II is slightly, but not much, more advanced. Nos. III and IV are among the most advanced that I can find. A really satisfactory exercise book would require the co-operation of a board of editors. I am not well enough read; and I find to my discomfiture that most of the examples that occur to me hardly rise above the simplicity of No. I. Numerous advanced exercises are possible to those who possess a familiarity with foreign languages.

I

'The barbaric sense of the exceeding sinfulness of sin,
with the moral hatred it carried, is giving way to a more
natural attitude. Vice offends more from its ugliness than
from its sinfulness/ Goodness has its appeal in moral beauty
rather than in virtue/—JOHN A. HOBSON: *The Moncure
D. Conway Lecture* 1933.

II

'At the end of my life as a teacher . . .. I am convinced
that it is personality that counts always and all the time. . . .

'This question of Latin is a part, and only a part, of what
I think is the most important educational question that is
now before the country. It is a question which is engaging
the attention of the Consultative Committee of the Board
of Education at the present moment—the question of what
is the right education to give pupils between the ages of
11 and 16½, whose education is not going to be continued
beyond that point. Are we giving the right education at
the present time? I am pretty certain that we are not.

'I would give a boy first a sound education based on
English culture, English geography, English history, and
English literature, less mathematics, a different kind of
science, and I would not attempt to teach him more than
one foreign language. I would also try to give him a thorough physical education, and a thorough training of the
hand, eye and ear, and I would seek to make that as important as his literary education. In his last years at school
I would seek to build on that foundation some under-

standing of the modern world, why it is, how it works, and what his place is in it. In that education I do not think that there will be room or time for Latin, but at present we have not formulated anything like that. It is still an ideal.'—DR. CYRIL NORWOOD, addressing the Conference of the Incorporated Association of Preparatory Schools at the Hotel Great Central, Marylebone (*The Times* newspaper of December 21, 1933.)

III

'Character, in short, is an impersonal ideal which the individual selects and to which he sacrifices all other claims, especially those of the sentiments or emotions. It follows that character must be placed in opposition to personality, which is the general-common-denominator of our sentiments and emotions. That is, indeed, the opposition I wish to emphasise; and when I have said further that all poetry, in which I wish to include all lyrical impulses whatever, is the product of the personality, and therefore inhibited in a character, I have stated the main theme of my essay.'—HERBERT READ: *Form in Modern Poetry*, pp. 18-19.

IV

'Any serious criticism of communist philosophy must start by declaring openly how much of its theory is accepted by the critic. I must therefore preface my criticism by saying that I accept the rejection of idealism and the principle of the unity of theory and practice in the sense in which I have expounded it. And since this is the truly revolutionary principle, such an acceptance involves taking

one's stand within the tradition of thought which deri
from Marx. The negative implications of accepting tui
fundamental principle go very deep. They include the
rejection of all philosophy and all social theory which doe
not accept this principle, not because of particular objec·
tions to their conclusions, but because of a complete bre
with the assumptions upon which they are based and th,
purpose which governs their development. They involv
the belief that all theory must seek verification in actioᵣ
and adapt itself to the possibility of experiment. Th·
make a clean sweep of speculative thought on the grour.
that the validity of no belief whatever is capable of demoı
stration by argument. They involve a refusal at any po
to make knowledge an end in itself, and equally, the rejᵢ
tion of the desire for certainty which is the motive gove
ing speculative thought.'—JOHN MACMURRAY: ′
Philosophy of Communism, pp. 62-63.

WS - #0067 - 110822 - C0 - 229/152/4 - PB - 9780243466580 - Gloss Lamination